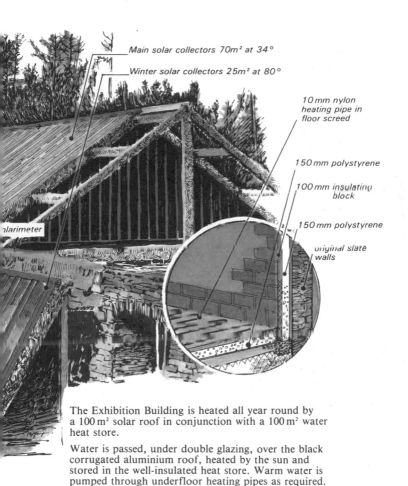

Main solar collectors 70m² at 34°

Winter solar collectors 25m² at 80°

10 mm nylon heating pipe in floor screed

150 mm polystyrene

100 mm insulating block

150 mm polystyrene

original slate walls

olarimeter

The Exhibition Building is heated all year round by a 100 m² solar roof in conjunction with a 100 m² water heat store.

Water is passed, under double glazing, over the black corrugated aluminium roof, heated by the sun and stored in the well-insulated heat store. Warm water is pumped through underfloor heating pipes as required.

The thermal performance of this building is being continuously monitored.

Reserve sources of energy and power as we know them, such as gas, oil and coal, will soon have been used up. In the not too distant future, energy for heat, light, transportation and industry will need to come from alternative sources. We cannot wait until we need them; alternatives for the future must be found now. This book describes what energy is, how we use it, how we waste it and what some of the alternatives might be.

Acknowledgments:

The photographs on pages 24 and 25 are reproduced by permission of the United Kingdom Atomic Energy Authority, and the diagrams on pages 46 and 47 were supplied by the Energy Technology Support Unit, AERE. Additional photographs and illustrations were supplied by the National Centre for Alternative Technology.

The illustration on page 38 is by Chris Reed and the front endpaper was drawn by Lynn N Grundy.

The illustrations on pages 10, 11, 12/13 and 30 are by Kathie Layfield.

First edition

© LADYBIRD BOOKS LTD MCMLXXXI

Energy

written by NIGEL DUDLEY
illustrated by PAT BORER

Ladybird Books Loughborough

WHAT THIS BOOK IS ABOUT

This book is about *energy* and the effect it has on our lives. It explains what energy is, where it comes from — and what we use it for. It describes how energy is produced today and how it may be produced in the future.

Energy is a very important subject at the moment because our traditional sources are beginning to run out and it is urgent that we find new ones. If we do not, we will face shortages in the future and this will mean hardship and unhappiness for many people. Sometimes we damage the environment when we use energy, by causing pollution and destroying areas of countryside that could otherwise be used for food production or leisure.

We will probably have less fossil fuel energy to use in the future. It is up to *us* to use it more efficiently so that everyone has a fair share and we must find the safest possible ways to produce enough energy.

As well as the fuel they use, remember the 'hidden' energy used in the manufacture of goods

25.1% Domestic
Heating, Hot water, Cooking, Lights etc.

14.2% Passenger Transport
Fuel, Vehicle construction, Sales, Garages. 25% Public, 75% Private.

100%

UK Fuel Input

30.2%
Fuel Industry
Absorbs nearly 30% of the fuel in processing and distribution.

4.7%
Clothing
Materials,
Shops,
Transport,
Advertising
Manufactur

Home
Building,
Furniture

5.6%

Luxury goods
Record players,
Cameras etc.

8.0% **Public Services**
Defence, Police, Health,
Government, Post

12.2% **Food**
Fertilizers, Fuel, Farms,
Making tractors, Shops

5

WHAT ENERGY IS

We need energy to keep us alive. Energy is the force that causes any change. It can occur in many different forms: as mechanical energy (movement), chemical energy, electricity, heat, light and sound.

Whatever the change is − the breaking of a cup, the blooming of a flower or the heating of a room − energy is necessary to make it happen. Energy is all around us and we use it all the time.

One important fact you should know about energy is that *one kind of energy can be converted to another.* For example, when gas is burned, the chemical energy stored in the gas is turned into heat and a small amount of light. Energy can never be destroyed but tends to degrade into low-level *heat* which is of little use. A great deal of our energy comes from the sun. The sun is a sort of nuclear reactor and gives off heat and light to the rest of the solar system. It is so enormous that it will continue to burn for millions of years.

ENERGY CAN BE CHANGED FROM ONE FORM TO ANOTHER

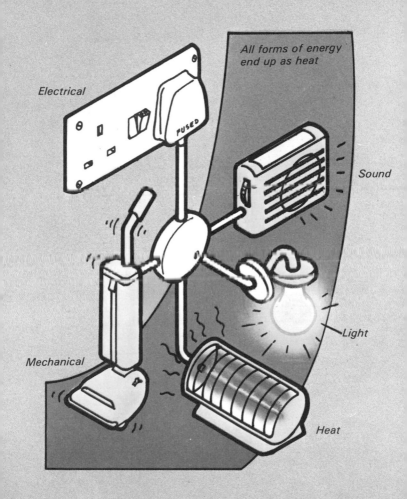

All forms of energy end up as heat

Electrical

Sound

Light

Mechanical

Heat

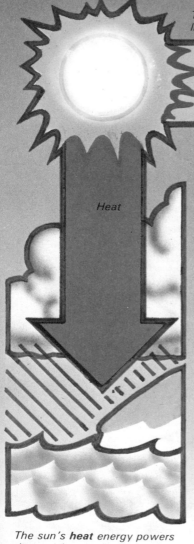

The sun's **light** energy powers living things

Light

Heat

HOW THE EARTH USES ENERGY

When the sun's energy reaches the earth, one third of it bounces straight off again and is reflected back out into space. However there is still enough left to provide our world with most of its energy. The sun *warms* the earth and gives us *light*. Some of the heat energy evaporates water, which rises through the air and forms clouds. These later produce rain. Warm air also rises and cold air moves in to replace it, causing winds to blow. Thus the heat from the sun provides the energy for our weather cycle.

The sun's **heat** energy powers the weather cycle

Plants

Chemical energy

Animals

   Some of the light energy is collected by plants and stored in their tissues. They later use this energy to grow and reproduce. Animals cannot collect the sun's energy for themselves, but need to eat plants and take the energy they have stored. All the energy for our bodies comes from eating plants, or eating animals that have eaten plants. In this way, the light energy from the sun gives living things their energy.

MAN BEGINS TO LEARN ABOUT ENERGY

Early man collected all the energy he needed by eating plants and animals. Later, as he learned more about the world around him, he found that there were other ways of using energy stored by living things besides eating them.

First, he discovered *fire*. When we burn wood, we release the sun's energy that has been stored by the tree, to provide ourselves with heat. Fire kept man warm and cooked his food. Later it was used to refine metals from natural ores so that more efficient tools and machines could be made, and a proper civilisation began to develop.

Next, man learned to use other animals to help him with his work. Strong animals (like horses, oxen or bullocks) can move faster and pull heavier weights than we can ourselves and they were used to speed up work and as a means of transport.

Later, using waterwheels and windmills, man used energy provided by the weather to drive machinery.

Windmill used for grinding grain into flour. To work efficiently, the sails of a windmill should face squarely into the wind. The top of the tower, carrying the sails, can be moved round to make this possible

11

THE BEGINNING OF
THE INDUSTRIAL REVOLUTION

The next important step in our use of energy did not come for thousands of years, but then it quickly changed our whole way of life. This was the discovery of *coal*.

Coal is made of fossilised plants and takes millions of years to form. The plants have been compressed so that the energy they have stored is concentrated into a smaller space. This means that a piece of coal contains much more energy than a piece of wood of the same size. This energy can be released by burning.

Typical street scene showing the effect of the huge increase in the use of coal to fuel the new factories and heat houses in the Industrial Revolution

Coal is obtained from open-cast mines or found underground and has to be dug out by miners who may have to tunnel for miles beneath the surface to find a good seam of coal. Their work is hard and dangerous and they may get diseases of the lung through breathing in too much coal dust.

When coal was found in Britain, it meant there was suddenly much more energy available. At the same time new machines were developed which needed this energy and factories were built all over the country. A new age of high production and high energy use had begun and this was called the *Industrial Revolution*.

However, there were some problems with coal. The thick smoke blackened buildings, caused terrible smogs and made people unwell. Soon people were complaining about the pollution caused by coal,

THE DISCOVERY OF OIL AND GAS

Fossilised plants can also form a thick black liquid called *oil*. This occurs in underground reservoirs and is often found with a natural gas. Both of these can be burnt to release heat energy in the same way as coal. Coal, oil and natural gas are known as *fossil fuels* because they all come from fossilised plant or animal material.

Oil is extracted by drilling a hole from the surface and pumping the liquid out of what is known as an *oil well*. Sometimes the oil is under pressure and spurts out when the drill reaches the reservoir, forming a fountain of oil called a *gusher*. A number of different oils can be refined from crude oil, including petrol, paraffin and diesel.

Oil was discovered in parts of the United States during the last century. Soon, large areas of the countryside were covered with tall towers called *derricks* that were used to drill for the oil. Many fortunes were made from the oil and towns grew up around the oilfields.

Much of the American oil is now used up and most of the world supply comes from the countries in the Middle East.

Britain extracts its own oil from the North Sea. This is especially difficult as the drills have to be mounted on huge platforms that stand on very long legs on the sea bed. For exploration purposes, drills are based on floating platforms which can be towed from place to place.

Natural gas

Oil

Typical North Sea oil derrick

15

WHAT WE USE ENERGY FOR

Within a few years of the introduction of oil and natural gas, people had far more energy than ever before. Today, in countries like Britain, we are used to having as much as we want, but fifty years ago many people relied far more on their own feet for transport and on burning wood to keep warm.

What do we use energy for today? Coal is mainly burnt in power stations to produce electricity. This provides energy for cookers, electric fires, television sets and food mixers — in fact anything that needs to be plugged into an electric socket.

Electricity is popular because it is very easy to use, but it is expensive to produce and a lot of coal or other fuel is needed to make a small amount.

Oil provides energy to drive engines, especially the *internal combustion engine*. Oil drives our cars, motorcycles, aeroplanes and ships and many of our trains — so our transport system relies on oil to keep it going.

However, like coal, oil produces harmful air pollution when it is burnt, and oil spilt at sea has damaged our beaches and killed thousands of sea birds.

Most gas is piped to people's houses and used for cooking and heating. All three energy sources, coal, oil and gas are used in industrial processes and to provide energy for heating.

Although fossil fuels are useful, the pollution they cause makes some people think that it would be better if we could find other ways of producing energy.

FUELS

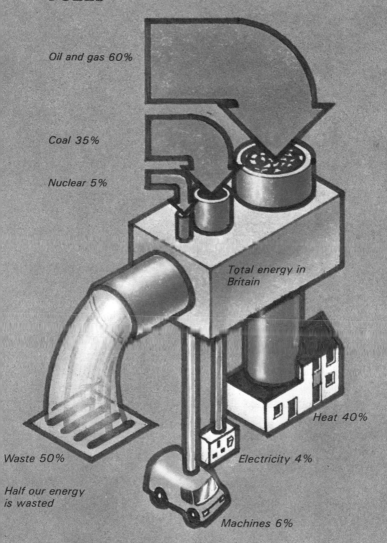

Oil and gas 60%

Coal 35%

Nuclear 5%

Total energy in Britain

Heat 40%

Waste 50%

Half our energy
is wasted

Electricity 4%

Machines 6%

FOSSIL FUELS ARE BEGINNING TO RUN OUT

As you can see, we rely largely on fossil fuels to provide us with the energy we need to live. If they were no longer available, there would have to be some very big changes in our way of life.

However, one day our reserves of fossil fuels *will* run out, and because they take so long to form, there will be no more available in the foreseeable future.

As this happens, we will have to switch gradually to other ways of producing energy. Although we still have coal left for a few hundred years, oil and gas could be in short supply by the end of the century. We have to act *now* to find alternative energy sources.

It is important that we use less energy and conserve our fossil fuels for as long as possible. Fossil fuels are not only used to provide energy but also as the raw materials in the manufacture of most plastics and man-made fibres. If these were no longer available it would have an enormous effect on our lives.

At the same time as using less energy, we have to start looking for alternative energy sources for the future. As fossil fuels become scarce and more expensive, we will be forced to take them from less accessible places. Oil is now being obtained from Alaska as supplies in the rest of America are running out and because the prices charged by Middle Eastern and other countries are high. This means that the oil costs more to extract and so becomes more expensive to buy.

Many poorer countries already have insufficient oil because they cannot afford to buy it. The days of cheap energy are numbered.

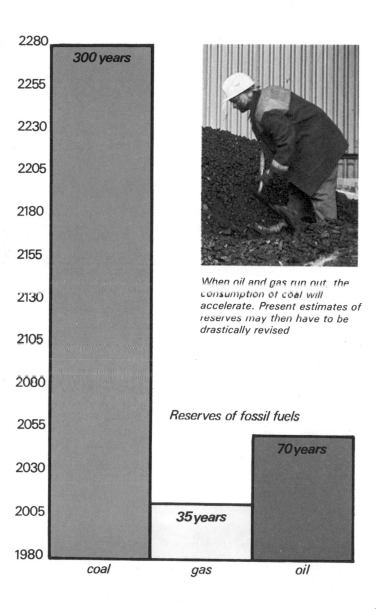

2280	*300 years*		
2255			
2230			
2205			
2180			
2155			
2130			
2105			
2080			
2055			
2030			*70 years*
2005		*35 years*	
1980	coal	gas	oil

When oil and gas run out, the consumption of coal will accelerate. Present estimates of reserves may then have to be drastically revised

Reserves of fossil fuels

NUCLEAR POWER

An alternative energy source is *nuclear power*. When the smallest part of an element (an atom) splits into a number of pieces, it releases very powerful forces as energy. It is normally difficult to split atoms, but some elements (for example uranium) are fairly unstable and can be broken up.

When an atom breaks and releases energy it is known as *nuclear fission*.

Nuclear fission was developed in the Second World War to produce the atomic bomb.

Nuclear power station

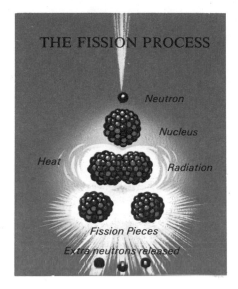

THE FISSION PROCESS

Neutron

Nucleus

Heat

Radiation

Fission Pieces

Extra neutrons released

When bombarded with neutron particles, the nucleus of a uranium atom is split into two pieces. This produces energy in the form of heat and radiation. Extra neutrons are also released so that the process is continued by a chain reaction

After the war scientists looked for peaceful ways to use nuclear fission. They found a way of converting the energy released into electricity, by breaking up uranium in a nuclear power station to produce heat which was then converted into electricity.

The first commercial nuclear power station was constructed at Calder Hall in Britain in 1956, and now they are built all over the world.

Uranium is dug or mined out of the ground, having been formed in the earth at its birth. In an operating reactor, uranium produces another element called plutonium which can also be used as a nuclear fuel.

Nuclear power stations use vastly less fuel to produce electricity than the fossil fuelled power stations, with less immediate effect on the environment. Although nuclear power can and will make a contribution to our energy supply, it does have its own problems.

SOME PROBLEMS OF NUCLEAR POWER

Nuclear power stations have been built all over the world and many more are planned. A more efficient reactor, called a *fast reactor*, means that supplies of uranium will now last much longer. On the face of it, nuclear power seems to be the answer to our energy problems.

Natural uranium is safe to handle but nuclear power is not as simple as it seems. Nuclear fission gives off dangerous *radiation* which can cause illness or even death, so any accident that releases this is very serious. So far no major accident has occurred, although there have been some very near misses, such as the accidents at Brown's Ferry and Harrisburg in the United States.

The radiation can last for thousands of years, so the waste from power stations has to be stored where it cannot leak for all that time. No one really knows how to store it; at the moment it is thought that the best method would be to amalgamate it with glass and to bury it in remote parts of the country, although the people living there are often strongly opposed to this. It is now thought that even small amounts of radiation, which used to be considered harmless, can also damage our health.

Even if we can make equipment very safe, we can never completely eliminate the factor of *human error,* and most accidents that have taken place in 'safe' nuclear power stations have been the result of a mistake. The fire at Brown's Ferry was started because workmen were testing for draughts with a lighted candle. We can never ensure that an accident cannot take place.

Although nuclear scientists are confident that they can solve the problems of radiation, they have not done so yet. Radioactive waste *has* leaked from power stations and storage dumps.

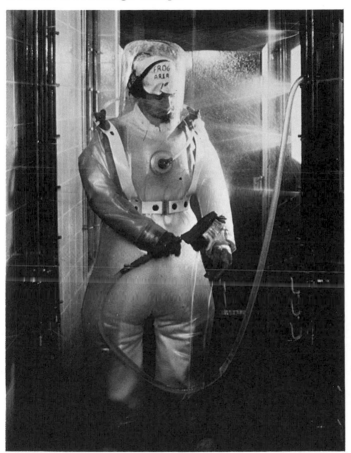

Man in a decontamination chamber washing his suit after working with radioactive materials

There is a great deal of argument about the safety of nuclear power. Some countries (like Austria) are looking for safer alternatives. Others are continuing to build nuclear power stations.

Even if we do use nuclear power, the supplies of uranium will not last for ever, so many scientists are looking at other ways of producing energy.

Another form of nuclear power is *nuclear fusion*. This means the joining together of two atoms, instead of the splitting that takes place in *fission*. Nuclear fusion also releases energy, and the *sun* is itself

The fast breeder reactor at Dounreay in Scotland

undergoing nuclear fusion continuously. Some scientists believe that nuclear fusion could eventually solve all our energy problems, because energy is released during the reaction. Nuclear fusion produces far less radioactivity than nuclear fission and so would probably be safer. Even the most optimistic researchers believe it will take many years and huge amounts of money to achieve a fusion reaction in a controlled situation. We cannot count on nuclear fusion solving our energy problems in the *near* future.

Hunterston 'A' reactor in Ayrshire, Scotland

THE FIRST STEP: SAVING ENERGY

Whatever happens in the future we will probably have less energy than we do at the moment and energy will be more expensive. It is important that we think of ways of *saving* energy so that we make better use of what is available.

We must think of where we waste energy and how we can reduce this waste. Look at the things you do and see how you can use less energy.

A common way to waste energy is to leave things like lights, radios, etc. switched on when they are not needed.

External wall insulation. One of the experiments being tried to reduce heat loss from old houses

SOME OF THE SIMPLE AND OFTEN INEXPENSIVE WAYS OF SAVING ENERGY IN THE HOME

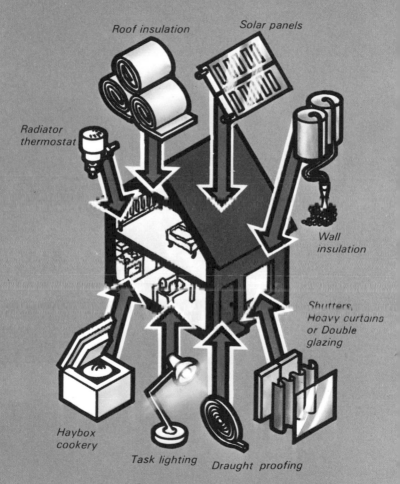

Roof insulation

Solar panels

Radiator thermostat

Wall insulation

Shutters, Heavy curtains or Double glazing

Haybox cookery

Task lighting

Draught proofing

The energy consumption of an average house could be drastically reduced by more appropriate and economic use of the energy we must use and by the retention of heat that, at present, is lost through poor insulation

MATCHING ENERGY USE TO NEED

Another way we waste energy is by using *more* than is needed to do a job.

This means using a big machine to do a job that could be done by a much smaller machine or by hand. Many luxury goods like dish washers or electric tooth brushes are like this. Although we may think that we must have them today, a few years ago no one used them and managed to clean their teeth and dishes quite satisfactorily.

In rich countries, *electricity* is often wasted by using it unnecessarily, or for jobs for which it is not suited. As we have said earlier, electricity takes a lot of fuel to produce, yet many people use this expensive form of energy for heating, instead of using coal in the first place. Electricity should be saved for jobs for which it is especially suited, like powering radios, motors or light bulbs. With modern methods of burning coal it is possible to extract much more of the available energy and to avoid most of the pollution that has caused so many problems in the past.

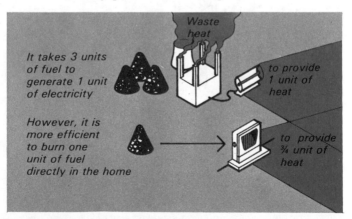

It takes 3 units of fuel to generate 1 unit of electricity

Waste heat

to provide 1 unit of heat

However, it is more efficient to burn one unit of fuel directly in the home

to provide ¾ unit of heat

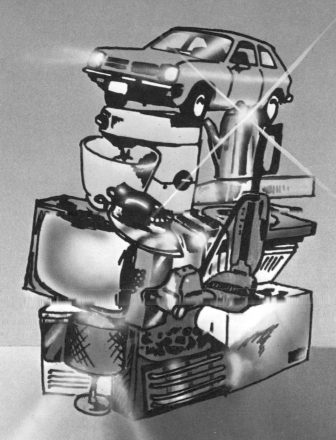

ENERGY GOBBLERS

Both in manufacture and use.
Are there low-energy alternatives?

KEEPING OUR HOUSES WARM

In our homes, most of the energy is used for heating. We have to heat the house itself and heat water for washing.

Many houses lose heat quickly through windows, walls and ceilings. Draughts of cold air blow in and lower the temperature and we have to use more energy to keep the house warm.

Draughts can be reduced by sealing gaps in windows and doors, using a special foam plastic tape and by blocking off disused chimneys.

Next, the heat must be kept in. To reduce heat loss from a building, special materials are used that do not allow heat to pass through them very easily — this is known as *insulation*.

The birds on the roof of this house are benefitting more from the heat than the occupants

In 1975, Wates, the building contractors, produced a house designed to reduce heat loss. It had features like smaller windows, insulated walls, floors and roof

As warm air rises, a lot of the heat will be lost through the roof, so the ceiling is insulated first as this is cheap and easy to do. The walls are then insulated and lastly the floor. Heat loss through windows is cut down by having thick curtains, or two layers of glass (known as *double-glazing*).

A well-insulated house can prevent a substantial amount of heat from escaping. If well designed in the first place, a modern house could lose only a fifth of the heat lost by non-insulated houses.

HOW WE WASTE ENERGY IN TRANSPORT

Another large energy user is transport. Most families have their own car and each car has to be fed continuously on petrol to give it the energy to move.

The advantage of having individual cars is that we can travel where we like, when we like. The disadvantages are that they use an enormous amount of energy, make a lot of noise, take up space for roads and garages, and the fumes from burning petrol cause pollution. On balance, it might be better if we could reduce the number of cars on the road.

For short journeys, we could use bicycles much more often. Bicycles are small, quiet and cause no pollution. Riding them would help to keep us fit and would reduce the huge traffic jams found in cities in the rush hours.

For longer journeys we could make much more use of public transport. Travelling by bus or train uses much less energy per person than if everyone drives their own car, and it is not as tiring. People say that public transport is too expensive, but they forget the money they spend buying their own car, and the cost of tax, insurance and road expansion schemes.

We would save a lot of energy and live in a more pleasant world if so many did not insist on having their own cars.

The diagram opposite shows the wastefulness of individual transportation. Increased use of public transport would reduce running costs and help to keep fares down

500 people can travel in

125 cars

10 coaches or

1 train or

SAFER WAYS OF PRODUCING ENERGY

After we have saved as much energy as we can, we still have to produce energy from somewhere.

When we burn fossil fuels, we are using the sun's energy that was collected millions of years ago and has been stored until now. Scientists today are looking at more direct ways of using the sun's energy (*solar energy*) without having to wait so long.

The diagram shows how we can do this. We can collect the sun's energy directly as heat and light, or as it is passed through the weather cycle as wind and water, or as it is collected and stored by plants.

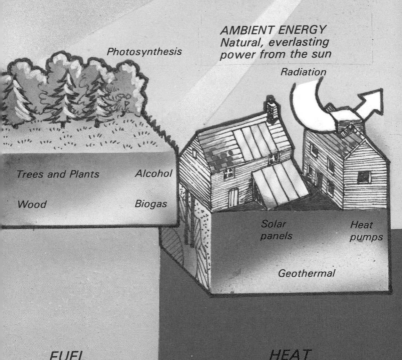

Photosynthesis

AMBIENT ENERGY
Natural, everlasting power from the sun

Radiation

Trees and Plants   Alcohol

Wood   Biogas

Solar panels   Heat pumps

Geothermal

FUEL   HEAT

We call these *renewable* energy sources as they are available for as long as the sun still burns, which will be many millions of years. We will look at some of these energy sources on the next few pages.

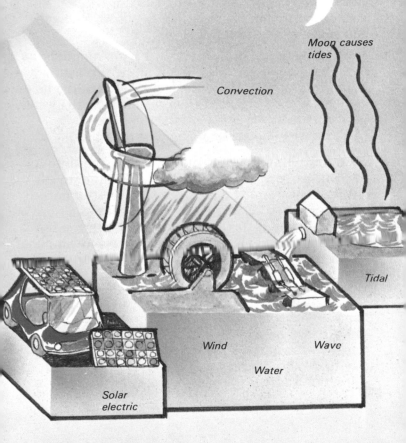

Moon causes tides

Convection

Tidal

Wind

Wave

Water

Solar electric

ELECTRICITY

USING THE HEAT OF THE SUN

One of the simplest ways of collecting solar energy is by using a *solar panel*.

To make a solar panel, we need a material that is a good *conductor* of heat. Most metals are good conductors and one that is often used is *copper*. The metal must have a black surface to absorb sunlight and convert it to heat.

A flat plate of blackened copper has a number of pipes fixed to it. The plate is left in the sun and it begins to heat up. Water is pumped through the pipes and heat energy is passed from the metal to the water, raising its temperature. Thus the sun's energy is collected by the plate and passed to the water.

To make it more efficient, the panel is put into a box with glass in front and insulation behind to cut down the heat loss. Solar panels work best in hot weather, of course, but they will still heat water even on cloudy days if the air temperature is not too low. An average family in Britain could expect to get about 40 per cent of their hot water needs in a year from solar panels.

Solar panels can be used to heat water for our homes. They are usually mounted on the roof. The sun can also be used to heat buildings all the year round, if the heat can be stored for long enough. One way to do this is to heat water in the summer and store it in a very well insulated tank for the winter.

Solar panels mounted on the roof to collect the sun's energy

CONCENTRATING THE SUN'S ENERGY

Although solar panels are good at heating water, they do not raise the temperature high enough for many industrial processes, or for cooking. To do this, we have to *concentrate* the sun's energy.

The commonest way of concentrating solar energy is to use a mirror curved into a *parabola*. This reflects all the light rays coming from the sun into a very small area so that the combined effect produces a high temperature. This is a similar principle to using a magnifying glass to concentrate the sun onto a point and make a 'hot spot'.

Parabolic mirrors need direct sunlight to work and are good for use in tropical countries where they are used to cook food. A huge parabolic mirror is used as a furnace in the mountains in France where it reaches temperatures of about 4000°C.

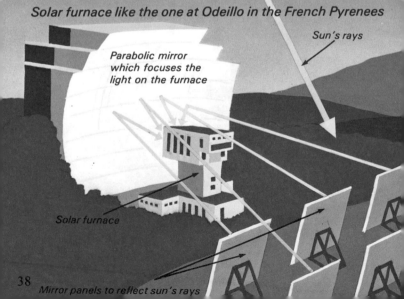

Solar furnace like the one at Odeillo in the French Pyrenees

Sun's rays

Parabolic mirror which focuses the light on the furnace

Solar furnace

Mirror panels to reflect sun's rays

Solar electric cells

In the United States and parts of Europe, experimental *solar power stations* are being built, working on a similar principle but on a much larger scale again. These may eventually be able to provide all the energy for a sizeable town or part of a city.

The second way of using solar energy directly is by converting light energy into electrical energy in *solar electric cells*. These were developed for the space programme and are used on satellites orbiting the earth. They are still very expensive and are only suitable for special jobs, like powering marker buoys out at sea, or radios up in the mountains. However, a new method of preparation has meant that the price has dropped considerably, and they may eventually be in much more common use.

ENERGY FROM THE WEATHER: WATER POWER

Falling water contains energy that can be used to drive machinery or produce electricity.

Water wheels are pushed around by the pressure of water on buckets or paddles attached to the wheel. They are useful for driving machinery and at one time many factories were built next to rivers so that they could be used. A watermill was a central point in a village or small town, where people would come to buy their flour.

Modern water turbines generate electricity. Water is piped downhill at increasing pressure to drive the turbine wheel or 'runner' which is enclosed in a steel case. The 'runner' shaft is connected to a generator which converts the mechanical energy of the wheel to electrical energy. This is known as *hydro-electric power* (HEP).

Watermill where the paddles are turned by the natural flow of water

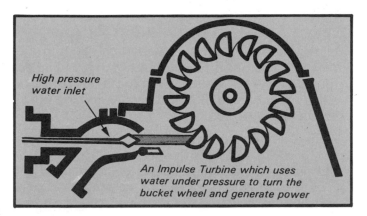

High pressure water inlet

An Impulse Turbine which uses water under pressure to turn the bucket wheel and generate power

In Britain we have concentrated on large scale schemes, where water is stored in man-made lakes and piped to a generating station below. The flooding of farmland is only partly compensated for by increased leisure use like fishing and sailing.

Although most large sites have now been developed, there is still plenty of scope for using streams and small rivers to provide electricity for a house or small village. This used to be done in days gone by, but was abandoned when cheap fossil fuels became readily available. It is now difficult to do this without paying a very high rate to the Water Authority, and many people believe this law should be changed to allow these energy sources to be widely used again.

Hydro-electric power stations are also sometimes used as 'pumped storage stations'. Large coal and nuclear power stations cannot easily be 'switched off' at night, but there is far less energy needed when most people are asleep. This spare energy can be used to pump water to a reservoir and can be used the next day to *produce* energy. Thus the energy can be *stored* as water kept in a high place.

ENERGY FROM THE WEATHER: WIND POWER

Old fashioned windmills collected energy from the wind and used it to drive machinery for grinding corn or pumping water. Modern wind machines convert the mechanical energy to electrical energy and are now called *aerogenerators*.

Aerogenerators come in many different shapes and sizes, but the principle is the same in all of them. Wind pushes the carefully shaped blades around and these are connected to an electric generator. A gearbox is usually needed to make the generator spin fast enough.

Some aerogenerators are quite small and can only charge a battery or provide lighting for a house. Others are much larger and produce enough electricity for a group of houses, or a small village. One of the largest aerogenerators in the world is the Tvindmill in Denmark and is 50 metres in diameter. It was built by a school to provide themselves with electricity and produces 2 megawatts (MW), which is enough to work 2,000 electric fires or about 35,000 light bulbs. Many countries are now building windmills producing several MW. A 3.7 MW windmill is being built in Scotland.

If we were to build many aerogenerators of this size they would soon be a common sight in the country and some people think they would be an eyesore. One suggestion for keeping them out of sight is to put them in groups in shallow sea areas where they would not be in the way and would catch plenty of wind. Even on this scale they would produce only a small proportion of our energy needs.

A typical modern aerogenerator

COLLECTING THE ENERGY STORED BY PLANTS

We can burn timber to heat our houses, especially if we use efficient wood burning stoves instead of the old fashioned open fire which allows a lot of the heat to go up the chimney. However, most countries are now running short of trees and many more will have to be planted if we are to use them as an energy source in the future. In Britain it is impossible that enough land could be found to grow even a fraction of our energy supply in this way.

There are two other common ways of releasing the energy stored in plants.

The first is a process called *distillation*, when alcohol is extracted from plant remains. We drink some kinds of alcohol, but another sort, called *ethanol*, can be used to replace petrol in cars. Brazil hopes to get all her transport fuel by distilling sugar beet to produce ethanol.

The second way is to let plant remains or animal manure (which contains plant remains) rot in a container which excludes oxygen. The species of bacteria that live in these conditions release *methane gas* as they break down the remains. This can be collected and burned to provide heat for houses or cooking, or to produce electricity in a generator.

This is especially useful, because the breakdown process kills most of the bacteria, and the resulting *slurry* can then be used on farmland as fertilizer. There are over seven million small methane digesters in China and half the cooking gas in rural areas comes from these.

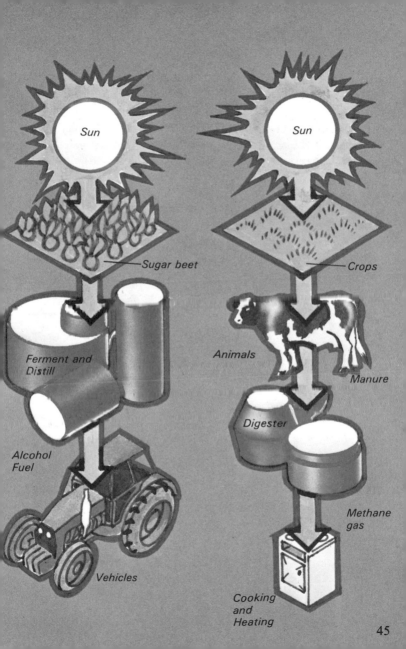

Sun

Sun

Sugar beet

Crops

Ferment and Distill

Animals

Manure

Digester

Alcohol Fuel

Methane gas

Vehicles

Cooking and Heating

45

ENERGY FROM THE OCEAN

Much of the earth's surface is covered by ocean, yet we have made little use of the energy it contains.

The rise and fall of the tide can be used to collect some of this energy. The tide coming into a bay or estuary is held back by a dam when the rest of the sea level falls again. This water then drives a turbine and generates electricity as it flows down to the lower tide level. A tidal power station built in France generates 240 MW, which is over 100 times more than the big windmill described earlier.

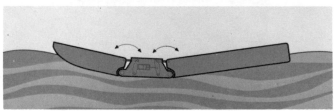

Cockerill's raft

Another exciting possibility is to collect the energy from the bobbing motion of the waves. Although

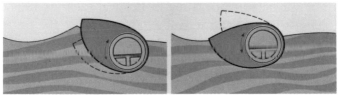

Salter's ducks

there are no large scale systems for doing this yet,
there are several experimental machines already
working. One of these involves the use of specially
shaped hollow blocks of concrete (called 'ducks') that
rock with the waves and collect energy. Rows of
ducks would be joined together out at sea and the
energy brought ashore by sending it along electric
cables.

The largest scale use of the sea as a power source
may be the eventual harnessing of the temperature
differences at various levels of tropical seas by means
of a *heat exchanger* but there is still a long way to go
in developing this idea. The USA hope to have a full-
scale plant in operation in 1985.

GEOTHERMAL ENERGY

Beneath the earth's crust there is a molten layer that is extremely hot. The earth has been cooling down ever since it was formed and will continue to do so for millions of years to come. As it cools, heat escapes to the surface and this energy can be used by man.

Occasionally, the molten material escapes directly to the surface as volcanoes or hot springs. The energy in hot springs has been used for some time in countries like Iceland and New Zealand where they are common. The hot water is used for washing and to heat radiators in people's homes. A power station run on water from a hot spring was operating in Italy as early as 1904.

The further down into the earth you go, the hotter it gets. Recently, work has been taking place to find ways of catching some of this heat where there are no hot springs. One method is to bore two holes far down into the earth's crust, and to circulate water through them, so that it heats up and carries the heat to the surface.

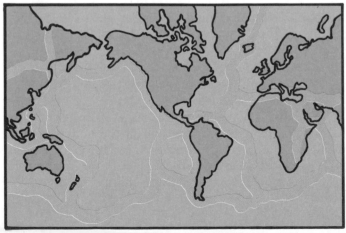

Red bands show areas of the world where geothermal energy is readily available

Water is pumped down to a hot rock region and used for district heating schemes

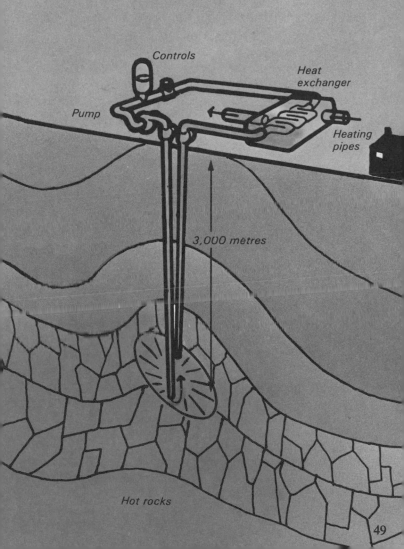

Controls

Heat exchanger

Pump

Heating pipes

3,000 metres

Hot rocks

THE FUTURE

At the moment, only a few people use solar panels and windmills. These are often enthusiasts who make their own equipment and like experimenting and finding alternative ways of collecting energy.

However, more and more people are becoming interested, and firms are beginning to make and sell the equipment needed. One day we may all be using some energy from renewable sources. This would mean a few changes in our lives.

A world using renewable energy sources would be much more varied than the one we live in at the moment. There would certainly be less pollution, and less danger of large scale accidents or disasters. Jobs would probably be less centralised, which means that they would be more evenly spread out over the country. People would tend to live nearer to their work, so would feel more part of the community and would know more people around them. We can hope that a more stable source of energy would help lead to a more stable society, and a happier life for us all.

We can start by wasting less energy ourselves and encouraging other people to do the same. We can join voluntary organisations that are interested in safe ways of producing energy and help them with their work. We must remember that our problems with energy are only part of a larger environmental problem of pollution, over population and lack of food. None of these aspects can be solved on its own, as they are all connected in various ways.

If we work together now, we could solve these problems and make our world a more pleasant place to live in.

A Darrieus aerogenerator being set up.
These may become a familiar sight in the future

INDEX

page

Accidents　　　　　　22, 50
Aerogenerators　　42, 43, 51
Alcohol　　　　　　　　44
Animals　　9, 10, 11, 44, 45
Atomic bomb　　　　　20
Atoms　　　　　　　　20

Calder Hall　　　　　　21
Chemical energy　　　6, 9
Coal　　12, 13, 18, 19, 28
Cockerill's raft　　　　46

Distillation　　　　　44, 45
Double glazing　　　27, 31

Electricity　6, 16, 17, 21, 28,
　　　35, 40, 41, 42, 44, 46
Energy:
　Alternatives　18, 20, 24, 50
　Conversion of　　　　6
　Renewable　　　　35, 50
　Saving　　　　　26, 27
　Shortages　　　　4, 18
　Waste of　17, 26, 28, 32, 50

Factories　　　　　　13
Fire　　　　　　　　10
Fossil fuels　4, 12, 14, 18, 19,
　　　　　　　　34, 41
France　　　　　　38, 46
Fuel　*see Fossil fuels, Coal, Oil*
　　　　　　　and Gas

page

Gas, Natural　14, 15, 16, 17,
　　　　　　　18, 19
Geothermal energy　　48

Heat　　　6, 7, 8, 10, 34
　Conductor　　　　36
　Exchanger　　　47, 49
　Loss　　　　　30, 31
　Low level　　　　6
Hot springs　　　　48
Houses　　　　16, 30, 31
Hydro-electric power
　　　　　　(HEP)　40

Industrial Revolution　12, 13
Industry　　　　5, 16, 38
Insulation　　26, 27, 30, 31

Leisure　　　　　　41
Light　6, 7, 8, 9, 28, 34, 38, 39

Machines　　10, 13, 17, 40
Mechanical energy　6, 40, 42
Methane gas　　　44, 45
Middle East　　　14, 18
Mines　　　　　　13

Nuclear:
　Fast reactor　　　22
　Fission　　　　20, 21
　Fusion　　　　　24
　Leaks　　　　22, 23
　Neutrons　　　　21